THE GRATER GOOD

KOA PRESS

THE GRATER GOOD

Flip Grater

Hearty, delicious recipes for plant-based living

PHOTOGRAPHY AND STYLING
BY TONIA SHUTTLEWORTH

KOA PRESS

CONTENTS

01/
/Intro

Kia ora! Bonjour!

Welcome into our kitchen.

Youssef and I met at 2 am on a cold September night in Paris in 2012. I was recording my album *Pigalle*; he was working in a famous jazz bar. As Montmartre closed, my bass player Seba let out his famous hearty chuckle, lifted a finger into the air and said, 'I know a place... the party will continue!'

We traipsed up and over the hill with our double bass and inappropriate footwear and arrived to Youssef's smiling face leaning over a balcony. He threw down a key, invited us up, immediately poured a round of whiskies and we settled in. There, nestled into a deep armchair under a large black and white photo of Camus, surrounded by stacks of old books and golden Moroccan trinkets, we discussed the meaning of life, and made plans to save the world.

Food and music were always the binding agents. I toured the world collecting recipes from my audience members and wrote recipe-laden tour memoirs. It allowed me to be constantly discussing food and wine and music with everyone I met. It was my first experience of bobo life on those and subsequent tours ... tasting the best wines across Europe, singing with the best punks and crooners, eating the most exquisite food everywhere we went. All whilst sleeping in dirty old venue apartments, running to catch trains, wearing vintage polyester dresses and heels worn down to nails.

By 2018, Youssef and I were living in New Zealand with our daughter Anaïs. My new domestic life and breeder-based fears for the future had me wanting to do more for the planet than writing sad songs. I wanted to promote plant-based eating full-time, not through protesting or education, but via the pleasant, delicious activism that came to be called Grater Goods. We made a chorizo out of beans and sold it on social media. I rented a small kitchen in an industrial part of Christchurch and cooked there three days a week. I made deli sandwiches for workers in the area and plant-based pilgrims who could find me. The demand grew so rapidly that within a year we'd taken over the whole building, with a team of staff and a bustling retail and hospitality space.

A little slice of Paris in industrial Sydenham. A fully plant-based menu of European-inspired deliciousness. Showing everyone who walks in the door that we no longer have to choose between pleasure and principles. And voila! Here we are now... still staying up all night, discussing the meaning of life and trying to save the world.

These recipes are edible activism, ethical hedonism. They're mostly unfussy, unpretentious and shareable. So please share them. Gather around tables, break bread and leave a ton of crumbs like the French do.

Alors, Bon ap!
Enjoy.

Flip x

Kitchen staples

I don't want to be a wanker about ingredients. I also want to recognise the fact that some good quality ingredients can be more expensive than their counterparts and therefore not available to everyone. That said, here is a rundown of my favourite ingredients in case it is at all helpful.

Salt

All my measurements are made using iodised flaky sea salt. If you switch to a fine salt it will be too salty so halve the quantity, taste the food, and add more until it is good.

Oil

I use a lot of extra virgin olive oil in this book because I buy it in enormous food service tins and choose that over every other luxury. You can substitute for any oil in any recipe but focaccia. Please don't do that to focaccia. For very simple recipes like white bean and garlic soup be aware that the quality of your oil will make a difference to the taste. Note that coconut oil cannot be substituted for another oil. In bocconcini (page 44) or mascarpone (page 214) for example, it's important because it solidifies when cool.

Pepper

Freshly ground black pepper is kind of key to some of these recipes. As is white pepper. They're very different and not interchangeable. White pepper has a kind of weird goat-smell vibe which adds funk, umami and warmth. Black pepper adds bright pops of heat and tart richness.

Beans

I haven't soaked a dry bean since the '90s. Cans are the easiest packaging to recycle and canned beans are perfectly delicious. Plus the liquid in a can of beans is an ingredient in its own right, called aquafaba. Some recipes will benefit from using all or some of this liquid, others will work better with drained, washed beans. Basically, this liquid is a binding agent, similar to the protein in eggs, so don't throw it away without considering whether to use it in a recipe or not.

Nuts and seeds

We all know we need more greens, nuts and seeds in our diets but raw nuts sprinkled over steamed greens is no one's happy place. I've tried to showcase some of the incredible things you can do with nuts and seeds throughout your cooking in the pages before you. From adding crunch to salads, through to soaking and blending for cheeses and creams. Always buy in bulk, and try to get your hands on broken cashews as they're miles cheaper.

Cauliflower

Along with nuts, seeds and white beans, cauliflower is the best way to achieve creaminess. It's insane how decadent cauliflower can be when treated right. Just make sure it's nice and fresh.

Mushrooms

Anyone who knows me knows I'm obsessed with fungi. Mushrooms are an absolute staple in our home. Super nutritious, umami-as, and free if you know where to look! When pan frying your mushrooms, weigh them down with a second heavy pot. The best way is to cook between two cast iron pans. You'll get the most incredible texture cooking this way and you'll never look back.

Tofu

Tofu is genius. It's literally the original vegan cheese. It's incredibly versatile, delicious and completely under-utilised in European cookery. You can use firm tofu for any of the recipes in here. Silken tofu will also work for any blended recipes, just adjust the water accordingly.

Garlic and onion powder

Sometimes, when using the fresh product, these are interchangeable but mostly they're not. We use these because sometimes you need a dry ingredient but want the flavour of aromatics, and truly they give a more savoury flavour than the fresh option; there is more umami and depth. Do not use onion salt or garlic salt – it is not the same thing.

Puff pastry

Store-bought puff pastry is awesome. Dairy-free versions are widely available and not always labelled as dairy-free, just check the ingredients.

Flours

Chickpea flour, gluten flour and wheat flour are not interchangeable. Chickpea flour is yellowish and should be whisked or sifted into things as it tends to clump. Gluten flour (or wheat protein) is wheat flour that has had the starch washed away, leaving a super high protein flour. It's available in specialty stores and online. If you can't get your hands on it, you can rinse wheat flour under water until you're left with a gloopy, stringy mess which is pure gluten. Cornstarch/cornflour can be subbed with potato starch or tapioca starch.

Milks

I use mostly organic, unsweetened soy milk. It's the right mix of fatty, delicious and sustainable for me. It's the best option for mayo or aioli due to the protein level. I also recommend oat milk for general use. You can use any other plant milk you like – hemp, almond, rice all work perfectly fine. Coconut milk is the fattiest and has a strong flavour so is best for desserts.

Stock

Seriously, who has time to make stock from scratch? This is up there with homemade pastry in my world. I tend to use an Australian stock powder called Massel, who do a range of meat-free chicken and beef stocks but there are many great vegetable stocks around. For mushroom stock I use shiitake stock (widely available at Asian supermarkets) or simply the soaking liquid from rehydrating dried mushrooms.

Soy sauce and tamari

You'll notice I use these quite a bit throughout the book. They are both made from fermented soybeans to create a salty liquid used in cooking to achieve a rich, umami flavour. Tamari is mainly gluten-free and less salty, while soy sauce is the saltier of the two.

High-speed blender

The most used piece of equipment in our kitchen! I recognise that a bunch of recipes call for a good blender. A bullet blender does an amazing job and you can get these relatively cheaply, however investing in a good high-speed blender, particularly one with a tamper, is totally worth it if you're planning to make a lot of plant-based foods.

Mortar and pestle

While we have all seen the marble ones and small wooden options, if you're going to get one, get a large durable one that can hold a decent amount. Smashed food tastes great and is fun.

Knives

Here is the difference between enjoying cooking and despising cooking: a good knife.

Unusual ingredients

Some of these ingredients will be unfamiliar but they're all worth knowing about and can change your pantry and cooking forever.

Nutritional yeast

I admit this is a weird ingredient. Those in the know call it 'nooch'. It is not interchangeable with brewer's yeast or active yeast or any other type of yeast. It's yellow and flaky and if you can't find it at local specialty stores, try online, otherwise omit. If you're new to this ingredient, be warned, it's addictive. Once you've had hot popcorn coated in this you won't eat popcorn any other way.

Liquid smoke

This delicious witchcraft is strong and bitter but used sparingly can add so much to a dish. It's especially effective in vegan meats and is a great way to cheat some smoky flavour into things without setting off the smoke alarm in your apartment building (been there, done that).

Agar agar

Also known as agar flakes or agar powder. Made from algae, this works as a non-gross gelatine (setting agent) in sweet and savoury dishes. Make sure you wash all pots and utensils quickly after working with this as it sets.

Nori sheets

Since we're talking about seaweed, let's discuss nori. Commonly used for sushi, this is easy to find and adds an ocean vibe to your food. Cut with kitchen scissors or tear with your hands. There are some other amazing ocean weeds out there but this is a nice gateway algae. We can get into kelp in the next book!

Xanthan gum

This is a thickening agent and can be widely found. It can be left out of recipes, you'll just get a different texture.

Flaxseed

A great way to get omegas without seafood, flaxseeds can be eaten whole or ground into a powder. When it's ground you can add water and create a binder (similar to egg) for baking. You can also make an 'egg' by adding water to whole chia seeds.

Black salt

Also known as kala namak, this salt is ironically pink in colour and smells of sulphur. Used sparingly it adds an eggy taste to dishes but the flavour can dissipate so add near the end of cooking. Find it at Indian supermarkets or online.

TVP (textured vegetable protein)

A dried, soy-based product available in specialty stores and some supermarkets. The finest kind is similar in size to mince meat – this is the most versatile type. It's also available in larger chunks which can be soaked in marinade and used in stir-fries, cassoulets, tagines etc.

Gluten flour

A wheat flour that has had the starch washed away, leaving a super high protein flour. It's available in specialty stores and online. Mainly used to make seitan (wheat gluten) but can also be added to 00 flour to create more stretch in pizza or bread dough.

Tapioca

Also called cassava starch, this is one of my favourite starches. It's used as a thickening agent for sweet and savoury things, as well as making pearls for bubble tea and at times, vegan caviar.

GLUTEN
FLOUR

NUTRITIONAL
YEAST

XANTHAN
GUM

BLACK
SALT

NORI SHEETS

FLAXSEED

TAPIOCA

AGAR
AGAR

LIQUID
SMOKE

TVP

02/
/Apéro

/ Ahhhh APÉRO! Our favourite time of day and the inspiration for everything that Grater Goods is. Both a noun and a verb, you can have, take, or go for apéro. It can begin any time between 3 pm and 5 pm and last between 1–5 hours. It is simply the act of stopping your day, having a glass of whatever and a snack prior to dinner, usually with others. /

Cashew Ricotta

This is a version of one of our classic cheeses created by our brilliant production manager Sonya. She's been with us since really early days and helped make Grater Goods what it is today. She's incredibly hard working, caring and hilarious and we love her.

SERVES 4

260 g soaked cashews
1 tablespoon nutritional yeast
1 teaspoon apple cider vinegar
1 teaspoon lemon juice
½ tablespoon flaky sea salt
1 teaspoon garlic powder
1 clove garlic
¼ cup water

A word on cashews:
Cashew pieces are ideal for a lot of this kind of recipe as they soften faster and they're loads cheaper. They will blend best if soaked overnight but if you're disorganised (like me) simply pour boiling water over raw nuts and leave for at least 10 minutes before blending.

Blend all ingredients in a high-speed blender, scraping the sides as needed. Chill and eat.

This is a basic dairy-free cheese recipe. It's super easy as it doesn't require draining with cheesecloth or culturing and can be used as a spreadable ricotta-style cheese. If you want a set cheese, simply put this mixture into a mould and freeze. Remove from mould and coat in cracked pepper, dried dill or chopped parsley and serve chilled.

French Onion Dip

This recipe was created by one of our genius chefs, Marshall. The key to any french onion recipe is to really spend the time to get your onions beautifully caramelised.

SERVES 1–2

300 g brown onion (approx 2
  medium onions), thinly sliced
1 tablespoon olive oil
100 ml white wine
1 tablespoon raw sugar
1 tablespoon wholegrain mustard
1 teaspoon flaky sea salt
100 g dairy-free cream cheese*
dill to garnish
vegan Parmesan to garnish

*We use Grater Goods Herb & Garlic Cream Cheese so if you're using a plain kind, taste and you may like to add garlic, herbs or salt as needed.

Heat oil over low heat and cook onion, stirring for 20 minutes, or until soft and brown. Be patient with this step, as it is where all the base flavour comes from. Add white wine and reduce until almost gone. Add sugar, mustard and salt and stir until sugar is melted. Take off the heat. Mix in the cream cheese.

Serve warm with crusty bread, topped with dill and Parmesan.

Potato & Rosemary Focaccia

This is ZERO EFFORT bread. I promise. It takes ages to proof but almost no time to make. And it can be simplified further by omitting the potatoes. I suggest making it when you wake up on the weekend and cooking it between 3-5 pm for apéro. Alternatively you can make it in the evening, leave the dough overnight at room temperature and bake it first thing.

SERVES 8 AS A SIDE

½ teaspoon active yeast
½ teaspoon raw sugar
2 cups luke warm water
3 cups all-purpose flour
¼ cup extra flour if needed
3 teaspoons flaky sea salt
1 medium waxy potato
a heap of olive oil
2 sprigs fresh rosemary,
    stalks removed

Combine yeast, sugar and water, mix and leave for 15 minutes until bubbles form and yeast has activated. Add 3 cups of flour and mix well. This will be a very wet dough or very thick batter – don't panic! Drizzle with a little olive oil, cover with a piece of compostable plastic or a wet tea towel and leave in a warm place for 2 hours. Sprinkle with 1 teaspoon of salt and 2 tablespoons of flour, pull together until you can knead it just a little to mix the salt into the dough. It will still be sticky but you should be able to handle it. Add a little flour if not.

Cover again and leave at least another 2 hours.

Preheat your oven to its hottest temperature (most probably 250°C). Thinly slice the potato. Boil covered in a little water and salt until partly cooked, about 2 minutes. Drain and set aside.

Tip your dough onto a baking tray lined with baking paper, try not to push all the air out! Mix 1 teaspoon of salt with 1 tablespoon of water. Dip your fingertips and press gently all over the focaccia, spreading to whatever shape you want.

Place potato slices onto your dough, sprinkle with the remaining teaspoon of flaky salt, a really good quantity of olive oil (at least 3 tablespoons) and rosemary.

Bake for 15-25 minutes until evenly golden and it smells awesome. Serve warm. This is best eaten on the day but if you keep it overnight just sprinkle with a little water and revive in a warm oven for 5-10 minutes.

Escarfaux

Our daughter Anaïs calls this 'mescargots' as in, my escargot! It's a great way to use wild mushrooms in autumn but can be made any time of the year with Paris button mushrooms. Serve with bread to mop up all those garlicky juices.

SERVES 4

8 medium button mushrooms
⅓ cup vegan butter (or dairy-free
   spread)
2 tablespoons olive oil
1 small shallot, finely sliced
6–8 cloves garlic, finely chopped
½ cup Chardonnay
½ cup vegetable stock
1 teaspoon white wine vinegar
1 sheet nori, cut into small pieces
sea salt to taste
pinch black pepper
bunch chopped parsley
crusty bread to serve

Cut mushrooms in half, then each half into 2 or 3.

Gently heat butter and oil in a pan, add shallot and garlic and warm for 30 seconds until fragrant. Add chopped mushrooms, wine, stock, vinegar, nori pieces, salt and pepper. Simmer for approx. 20 minutes, until the liquid has reduced substantially and thickened.

Taste and season if needed. Toss plenty of parsley through the mushroom mixture and serve immediately with crusty bread.

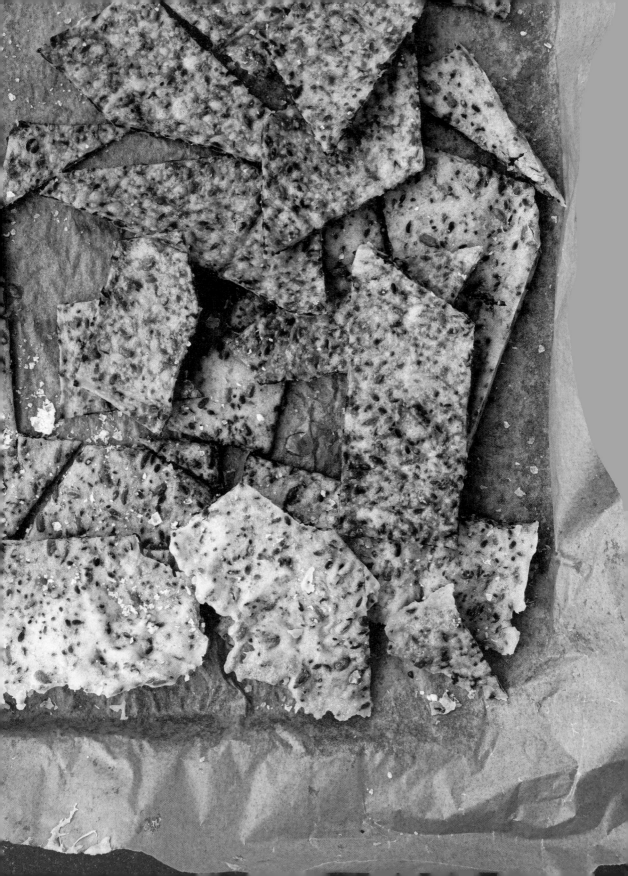

Super Seed Bark

1 cup gluten-free flour
1 teaspoon salt
¼ cup linseeds
¼ cup sunflower seeds
2 tablespoons chia seeds
2 tablespoons hemp seeds (switch out
    any of these for other seeds or even
    rolled oats as a cheaper option)
1 cup hot water
¼ cup rice bran oil

Line a baking tray with recycled baking paper and preheat oven to 170°C. In a bowl, mix dry ingredients together well.

Combine water and oil and add to the dry mix. Spread mixture as thinly as you can on the lined baking tray. It's a sticky mess at this stage but have faith! Use a wet spatula to spread as evenly as you can and don't worry about rustic edges. Bake for 10 minutes, then remove from oven and cut.

Place back into the oven for 50–60 minutes until golden. Allow to cool and store in an airtight container.

Italians are really the best at aperitivo – they'll put on such an epic spread that it becomes dinner. The French tend towards a more reserved apéro. It's still two hours long but it's most definitely a pre-dinner snack rather than a meal. But apéro is much more about the action of stopping than the accompanying food and drinks. It's about sitting alone or with friends and family, and marking the end of work or a pause in activities.

Mushroom & Hazelnut Pâté

SERVES 6-8

½ cup hazelnuts
½ large onion
2 cloves garlic
500–700 g mixed mushrooms*
2 tablespoons dairy-free margarine
1 teaspoon thyme leaves
1 teaspoon flaky sea salt
½ teaspoon freshly ground black
  pepper
2 tablespoons olive oil
pinch cayenne pepper
150 ml mushroom stock or
  vegetable stock
½ teaspoon agar agar
small handful of whole peppercorns

*I used a blend of wild mushrooms
– porcini, puffball and birch boletes.
Wild mushrooms will always give
a stronger, more complex flavour
but you can use button, shiitake –
whatever edible mushrooms you can
get your hands on.*

If you're using whole hazelnuts, crack open in a mortar and pestle and discard shells. You want about ⅓–½ a cup of shelled nuts. Spread on a tray and roast in a preheated oven for 10 minutes at 200°C until dark brown. Cover in a clean tea towel and rub to remove skins. Set aside.

Peel and roughly chop onion and garlic. Cut mushrooms into small cubes.

Heat margarine in a large frying pan, add onion. Fry for a few minutes until starting to soften, then add mushrooms, garlic, thyme, salt and pepper and cook down until mushrooms are soft and liquid has evaporated. Remove from the pan and leave to cool.

Place mushroom mix, toasted nuts and agar agar into a blender and blitz until smooth. If omitting agar agar you can leave it out here, just blend mushroom mix and nuts and serve the pâté in a jar or bowl.

If using agar agar:
Heat stock in a small pan until almost boiling. Add agar agar and stir continuously for 2–3 minutes to dissolve. Pour the liquid into your blender and blitz again with your pâté mix until well combined.

Crush a small handful of whole peppercorns in a mortar and pestle until half-crushed – you want some chunks rather than smooth powder. Spoon pepper into moulds and shake gently to coat the bottom. Gently spoon your pâté into the moulds, pressing and tapping to fill the space. Put into the fridge to set. Agar agar sets quickly but the flavours develop with time so ideally prepare it a day before serving.

Serve with cornichons and toasted bread.

Marinated Olives

200 g mixed olives
½ cup olive oil
1 tablespoon reserved olive brine
zest of 1 orange or lemon
1 teaspoon whole black peppercorns
4–5 cloves garlic, peeled
1 teaspoon sugar
4 cm piece of fresh rosemary or
    equivalent fresh thyme (alternatively
    ½ teaspoon dried herbs)

Drain olives and set aside, reserving a tablespoon of brine. Place all marinade ingredients into a bowl, mix to dissolve sugar. Add olives, combine well and leave to marinate in a sealed container at least overnight. Warm gently in a microwave or small pot before serving.

MAKING BOCCONCINI,
RECIPE NEXT PAGE.

Bocconcini

MAKES 6-8 BALLS

1 cup cashews (once soaked this
 will become 1⅛ – 1¼)
100 ml water
¼ cup tapioca starch
1 tablespoon nutritional yeast
2 teaspoons flaky sea salt
¼ cup coconut oil
juice of 1 lemon
1½ teaspoons agar agar

Soak cashews in enough fresh water to cover them overnight, or for at least half an hour in boiling water. Drain.

Place all ingredients except for the agar agar into a blender and blitz until very smooth. Taste and add salt if needed. At this point you have a liquid cheese.

If you're making pizza, simply pour a little cheese sporadically in circles on your base to create buffalo-style bursts of cheesiness. Or pour as a cheesy layer in lasagne.

To set into bocconcini balls:
Prepare an ice bath and 6–8 squares of plastic wrap.*

Pour the mixture into a heavy-based, non-stick pan. Add agar agar and heat gently, whisking continuously until starting to bubble. Switch to a silicone spatula and keep stirring to avoid the mixture sticking to the bottom, until it thickens and becomes stretchy. You'll notice it will start moving as one lump rather than a liquid. At this point take the pan off the heat and spoon a little of the mixture into the centre of a plastic square. Form into a ball and twist (or tie off) to hold in place.

Pop your wrapped ball into the ice bath and repeat with remaining mixture. If using ¼ cup of cheese for each ball you'll get 6 balls. Place the ice bath into the fridge and leave to set for at least 2 hours. Once set, remove plastic and place balls into heavily salted water (brine) and keep in the fridge for up to 10 days. (Mix 1 tablespoon of salt for every cup of water you use to make the brine.)

You can use anything strong and non-porous for this step. Compostable plastic wrap works great or reuse any kind of soft plastic or fabric you have – simply use small rubber bands to hold the spheres.

Carrot Lox

500 g carrots, peeled into long strips
4 teaspoons fine salt

Marinade:
1 sheet nori
1½ teaspoons flaky sea salt
¼ cup neutral oil (such as sunflower
    or rice bran)
1¼ teaspoons raw sugar
1 teaspoon liquid smoke
4½ teaspoons tapioca flour
pinch white pepper
½ teaspoon dried dill

Slice carrots as thinly as possible, a speed peeler works well. Sprinkle with salt, stir through, let sit for 30 minutes. Rinse and drain.

Blitz your nori sheet in a blender to make a powder (or cut into super small bits). Combine all marinade ingredients and pour over the carrots.

You can simply store this in your fridge and enjoy over a week or if you want to get fancy, you can gently sous vide* the carrots in the marinade. This just gets them super soft and silky and makes them fall apart in a manner closer to smoked salmon.

How to sous vide:
Place marinated carrots and marinade into vacuum bags and seal. Cook sous vide at 85°C for 2½ hours.

Home hack:
Simply place into a sealable bag. Put into a pot of cold water, bring to a simmer and turn off. They won't be silky but they will soften slightly.

Pickled Red Onion

By our fantastic chef Maki. We've had pickled onions on the menu forever but Maki made this particular recipe, which is SO delicious.

SERVES 10

2 cups white vinegar
2 cups water
1 cup raw sugar
½ cinnamon stick
2 star anise
5–6 large red onions

Put all ingredients except onions into a large pot. Heat until simmering, then turn off. Peel and finely slice onions. Pour hot liquid over the onions and keep in a sealed container in the fridge for 2–3 weeks.

Turmeric Pickled Courgettes

MAKES 2 X 270ML JARS

500 ml white vinegar
2 medium courgettes
½ red onion, finely sliced
2 tablespoons cheap salt (approx.)
4 tablespoons sugar
1 teaspoon whole peppercorns
2 teaspoons black mustard seeds
1 teaspoon ground turmeric
½ tablespoon flaky sea salt
1 teaspoon dried dill

Fill both jars to the top with vinegar and pour into a pot.

Cut your courgettes in half or quarters lengthways, then slice. Place with onion into a bowl, sprinkle thoroughly with salt, toss to coat and leave for 10–20 minutes. This will pull out some water from the courgette slices.

Rinse courgettes under cold water then leave to drain in a colander for 10–15 minutes. While these are draining, add sugar, peppercorns, mustard seeds, turmeric and sea salt to the pan of vinegar. Bring to the boil then turn down to a simmer for 10 minutes. Check your salt-sugar ratio by giving it a wee taste. Adjust if needed. Add dried dill.

Stuff the drained courgette pieces into your clean jars, top with hot pickling liquid, close lids tightly and store in the fridge.

These are delicious after 24 hours but best after a few days. Can be kept in the fridge for up to 30 days.

Pickled Mushrooms

SERVES 6

200 g button mushrooms, cut into
   halves or quarters.
5 tablespoons olive oil
⅓ cup water
⅓ cup white or red wine vinegar
1 large shallot, sliced
3 cloves garlic, peeled whole
½ teaspoon Dijon mustard
¼ teaspoon dried herbs (such as
   Italian mixed herbs or herbes de
   Provence)
1 teaspoon flaky sea salt
½ teaspoon raw sugar
¼ teaspoon black pepper
2 tablespoons fresh parsley, chopped
   (to garnish)

Add 3 tablespoons of olive oil and chopped mushrooms to a large, hot pan. Don't move the mushrooms too much – allow them to brown. Put all remaining ingredients (except parsley) into a bowl and mix to combine.

When your mushrooms have browned but aren't entirely cooked, pour the marinade over the mushrooms and let simmer for 2–3 minutes. Take off the heat and stir through the parsley.

Store mushrooms in the marinade in a sealed container at least overnight or up to 20 days in a fridge. You can also keep these in a sterilised jar, just top up with extra oil if needed.

MAKING ROSEMARY & SEA SALT CRACKERS,
RECIPE OVER PAGE.

Rosemary & Sea Salt Crackers

MAKES 2 OVEN TRAYS

¾ cup plain white flour
¾ cup plain wholemeal flour
1 teaspoon salt
½ teaspoon sugar
1–2 tablespoons nutritional yeast
1 tablespoon fresh rosemary, finely
   chopped
3 tablespoons olive oil
½ cup cold water
sesame or nigella seeds to garnish

Preheat oven to 200°C. Mix dry ingredients together. Add oil and water, mix until it forms a ball. Knead for 5 minutes. Split into two.

Roll out each piece onto baking paper until 2 mm thick then transfer to an oven tray. Prick all over with a fork, brush with a little water and sprinkle with seeds and salt flakes.

Cut into desired shapes. Bake until just starting to get brown, approx. 8–10 minutes at 200°C.

Allow to cool on tray, crackers will crisp as they sit. Keep in a sealed container for up to a week.

Petit Fours

Anything small and cooked in an oven, essentially. These super simple options are ideal for hosting or lunchboxes.

Mini Sausage Rolls
MAKES APPROX. 24

5 button mushrooms
1 small onion
1–2 cloves garlic
1 can black beans
½ teaspoon white pepper
2 teaspoons dried herbs
1 tablespoon soy sauce
1 teaspoon miso paste
1 teaspoon Vegemite (or 2
   teaspoons nutritional yeast)
salt to taste
2 tablespoons breadcrumbs
2 tablespoons oil such as
   sunflower or grapeseed
2 tablespoons wheat flour
3 tablespoons gluten flour
2 sheets dairy-free puff pastry

Roughly chop mushrooms, onion and garlic and fry in a little oil until softened and taking a little colour. Add to a food processor with beans, seasonings, breadcrumbs and oil. Taste and add salt if needed. Add both types of flour and blitz until mixture comes together. The mixture will be sticky but pliable. Leave to rest for 20 minutes.

Cut pastry into wide strips and place a line of your mushroom and bean filling across the centre. Fold the pastry over and seal with a little water.

Cut into bite-sized sausage rolls and spread across a lined baking tray, leaving space between each one. If the pastry has warmed significantly, place the oven tray into the fridge for 15 minutes so your little rolls are cool when they hit the oven. Preheat oven to 200°C. Brush sausage rolls with oil or plant milk and bake for 30–35 minutes until puffed and golden.

Lox Bites
MAKES APPROX. 30

1 telegraph cucumber
100 g dairy-free cream cheese
100 g carrot lox (page 48)
microgreens or sprouts to garnish

Cut your cucumber into rounds. Top with a little cream cheese and carrot lox. Top with garnish and serve. A super light vegan, gluten-free option for hosting.

Pesto Bows
MAKES APPROX. 50

100 g dairy-free pesto (page 204)
2 sheets dairy-free puff pastry

Preheat oven to 200°C. Spread pesto over rolled out sheets of pastry. Cut pastry into small oblongs, roughly 8 cm long. Twist each oblong in a full rotation, bringing the front surface around to face up again. Pinch the centre. Bake for 20–25 minutes.

Saucisse de Campagne

This was one of the first trials of vegan charcuterie we did. We love this – you can eat it as a charcuterie or fry it up as sausage.

MAKES 2-3 SAUSAGES

Dry:
1 cup gluten flour
2 tablespoons chickpea flour
2 tablespoons nutritional yeast
2 teaspoons mushroom powder*
    (optional)
2 teaspoons onion powder
2 teaspoons garlic powder
¼ teaspoon white pepper
2 teaspoons sea salt
1 teaspoon paprika
1 teaspoon ground coriander
½ teaspoon dried sage
½ teaspoon dried oregano
¼ teaspoon cayenne pepper
3 tablespoons adzuki beans

'Gristle':
200 ml vegetable stock
¼ cup TVP (textured vegetable
    protein

Wet:
½ cup coconut oil
¼ cup adzuki beans
1 teaspoon balsamic vinegar
1 tablespoon raw sugar
1 teaspoon tamari

*finely ground, dried shiitake
mushrooms*

Add all dry ingredients except beans to a large bowl. Mix well. Add beans.

For the 'gristle', combine stock and TVP, leave to soak for 20 minutes, then add to dry ingredients.

Place wet ingredients into a blender. Blend well, add to dry mix. Mix and knead the entire thing until you have a wet dough. Working with gluten flour is tough but work it well; knead for at least 10 minutes.

Form into sausage shapes, wrap in muslin cloth or tinfoil or a combo of baking paper and tinfoil. Make sure you twist or tie the ends well as they will expand. Steam sausages for 30-40 minutes.

Leave to rest in the fridge overnight. Enjoy sliced cold as a charcuterie or deli slice, or fry as a spiced breakfast sausage. Will keep in a sealed container for 10 days.

03/
/Entrée

/ I love an entrée. If you're not super hungry, it's enough.
If you're hosting, put out a bunch of entrées and call it dinner.
All these recipes could sneak into apéro snacks or mains,
depending on how they are served, and the salads and socca
are great picnic staples. If you want to do a staggered formal
meal any of these recipes would be great following antipasto
and prior to a main. /

Puy Lentil & Walnut Salad

This recipe is ALL about how you cook the lentils. As a general rule I use canned beans but will always cook lentils from scratch. They don't take too long and the difference is everything. Trust me - effort/reward ratio is the guiding force in my life.

SERVES 4 AS A SIDE

Lentils:
1 cup puy lentils (green or brown will
   also work)
3 cups cold water
1 shallot (or small onion) peeled and
   cut in half
2 cloves garlic, peeled
sprig oregano
sprig thyme
1 bay leaf
¾ teaspoon flaky sea salt

Dressing:
2 cooked garlic cloves
¼ teaspoon raw sugar
¼ teaspoon Dijon mustard
¼ teaspoon sea salt
1 tablespoon red wine vinegar
2 tablespoons olive oil

Salad:
cooked, seasoned lentils
½ cup walnuts, chopped
1 beetroot, finely sliced
150 g rocket (or mizuna or mesclun)
black pepper to taste

For the lentils, put all ingredients into a cold pan. Bring to a boil, cover and turn down to a good simmer, but be careful not to let it boil again. You want to keep some movement in the water without threatening to demolish the lentils. Check your lentils after 20 minutes. They may need 25–30 minutes total but you don't want them mushy. You want them soft with a tiny bite left so keep an eye on them and take off the heat when cooked. If they start falling apart at all, take them straight off.

Drain but don't rinse. Pick out the large parts of shallot/onion and herb stalks. Take the garlic cloves out and keep for the dressing. Set aside with lid on to keep warm while you make dressing.

For the dressing, combine all ingredients with the reserved cooked garlic, smashing the garlic with the back of a fork. Pour dressing over warm lentils. Leave to cool in a fridge for at least an hour, or overnight if you're uber organised and prepping the day before a party.

Combine your cooked lentils with all salad ingredients. Toss gently, taste a leaf and if needed, add sea salt and serve.

White Wine & Tarragon Fondue

If you've got a fondue set, use it but don't be put off if you don't! Just put it in a hot cast iron pot that will stay warm while you eat and use chopsticks, toothpicks, small tongs, whatever you like.

SERVES 4–6

¼ onion
1 medium potato
1 medium carrot
1½ cups soaked cashews
2 teaspoons garlic powder
2 teaspoons onion powder
2 teaspoons flaky sea salt
⅓ cup nutritional yeast
pinch black pepper
3 tablespoons oil (olive or
    sunflower oil)
1 cup unsweetened plant milk (soy
    or oat milk)
1 tablespoon tapioca starch
2 teaspoons lemon juice
⅛ teaspoon white pepper
¼ cup white wine
1 teaspoon dried tarragon

Peel and roughly chop onion, potato and carrot and boil all together in salted water until soft. Drain and add to a good blender.

Soak cashews for 10 minutes in boiling water. Drain, add to blender. Add all remaining ingredients and blend until very smooth. If it is too thick, add a touch of water.

Transfer to a pan and heat while stirring continuously, until bubbling. Pour into a fondue pan and serve with croutons.

Alternative versions:

Spicy Queso Fondue
Exclude the wine and tarragon and replace with:
1 tablespoon lemon or lime juice
5–10 pickled jalapeños
2 tablespoons jalapeño pickle juice
Serve with corn chips or toasted tortillas.

Smoked Pepper Fondue
Exclude the wine and tarragon and replace with:
1 roasted red pepper
1 teaspoon smoked paprika
¼ cup water
Serve with bread, croutons, radishes, tomatoes, cubes of cheddar... really anything.

Bruschetta

White Bean, Rosemary & Garlic
MAKES APPROX. 10

2 tablespoons olive oil
1 clove garlic, peeled and finely
  chopped
1 teaspoon rosemary, finely chopped
1 can cannellini beans
1½ teaspoons sea salt
a crack of black pepper

Add olive oil, garlic and rosemary to a cold pan. Heat gently until fragrant, add beans (with liquid), salt and pepper. Warm through and simmer gently for 5–7 minutes until most of the liquid has gone. Use the back of a fork to smash half the beans. Taste and adjust seasoning if needed. Schmear onto hot toasted bread.

Tomato Salad
MAKES 2

1 large tomato
½ teaspoon sea salt
1 tablespoon olive oil
a crack of black pepper
torn basil leaves
1 clove garlic, peeled

Dice tomato and add to a bowl with salt. Leave to sit for 30 minutes. Add all remaining ingredients except garlic. Rub garlic on freshly toasted bread, top with tomato salad and more fresh pepper.

Roasted Red Pepper Mess
MAKES 2

1 red pepper
6–8 olives
1 teaspoon capers
1 teaspoon caper brine
1 tablespoon olive oil
pinch salt and pepper
1 teaspoon red wine vinegar
½ teaspoon dried herbs
½ teaspoon sugar
1 teaspoon toasted pine nuts
  (optional)

Throw a red pepper into a hot preheated oven (200°C), turn once or twice and remove when soft and starting to blacken. Remove and place in a bowl. Cover to cool and steam for 10 minutes. Peel and discard the skin, remove the seeds and roughly chop.

Combine chopped roasted red pepper with remaining ingredients, mix well, taste, adjust seasoning, and leave to marinate for at least 30 minutes and up to 24 hours. Spoon onto freshly toasted bread.

Cauliflower & Black Truffle Soup

SERVES 4

½ onion, finely chopped
1–2 tablespoons low-flavour oil such
    as rice bran oil
1 teaspoon dairy-free margarine
2 cloves garlic, finely chopped
1 medium cauliflower, broken into
    large florets
1–2 cups vegetable stock (ideally
    a vegan chicken stock)
1 small Périgord black truffle or
    a drizzle of truffle oil

Sauté onion on a low heat in oil and margarine until transparent. Add garlic and cauliflower and a pinch of salt, stir for 2 minutes.

Add stock until the liquid just covers the cauliflower. Put lid on the pot and leave on medium temperature for 10 minutes or so, until the cauliflower softens.

Blend while hot. Check seasoning and consistency. You want it to be pourable, but comfortingly thick.

Serve in a bowl and top with as much black truffle shavings as you want. Alternatively, a few drops of truffle oil when serving will work, but don't overdo it. To serve, drizzle with olive oil (optional) and a load of freshly cracked black pepper.

Polenta Fries with 'Yolk'

This is a fun way to use up leftover polenta, as it works best with day-old polenta. You can also serve the 'yolk' with bread soldiers, or poured onto rounds of fried tofu to make egg-free fried eggs.

SERVES 6-8

Polenta Fries:
1 cup polenta, cooked
2–3 tablespoons olive oil
1–2 teaspoons dried Italian herbs

Yolk:
¼ teaspoon ground turmeric
2 teaspoons nutritional yeast
½ teaspoon black salt*
4 teaspoons cornflour
1 cup water
1 teaspoon lemon juice
1 teaspoon Dijon mustard
3 tablespoons sunflower oil

*Black salt or kala namak is, ironically, pink in colour. It's common in Indian supermarkets and specialty spice stores and adds an eggy (sulphuric) taste and smell to food.

Prepare creamy polenta from recipe on page 142 (You could simply cook polenta to packet instructions with water, but why would you when you could make it taste so good?)

Once you've stirred through the butter and Parmesan, pour cooked polenta into a square dish, spread evenly, cover and leave to chill overnight (or at least 4 hours).

Preheat oven to 220°C. Cut chilled polenta into roughly the size and shape of fries. Toss well in olive oil and dried herbs. Bake on a lined tray for 25–30 minutes, turning halfway through. Sprinkle with salt and serve hot.

Whilst fries are cooking, combine all yolk ingredients in a small pan. Mix well. Bring to a simmer, stirring regularly until thickened and combined. Taste and finish with a little sea salt or black salt. Serve warm.

Caesar Salad

SERVES 4–6

Tofu 'bacon' bits:
100 g firm tofu
2 tablespoons soy sauce
2 tablespoons maple syrup
2 tablespoons vegetable oil
1 tablespoon water
1 teaspoon smoked paprika
1 teaspoon salt
¼ teaspoon liquid smoke (or sub
   with extra smoked paprika)

To combine:
1 large cos lettuce
creamy cashew dressing (page 196)
tofu 'bacon' bits
croutons

vegan Parmesan to serve

Thinly slice tofu into strips. Place in a bowl and add remaining ingredients. Stand for at least 20 minutes to marinate.

Transfer both tofu and marinade to a non-stick frying pan and place over a medium-low heat. Monitor the heat as when liquid reduces the maple syrup is inclined to burn. Cook, turning halfway, for 6–8 minutes or until the liquid is absorbed, and tofu is golden and crisping on the edges. Transfer to a tray lined with baking paper and stand to cool to room temperature.

Grab two slices of sourdough (or whatever bread you have sitting around), cut into cubes and throw into the frying pan with a little olive oil for your croutons. Toss regularly until golden.

Wash and roughly chop lettuce. Dress with your creamy cashew dressing (you may need just half of it or all of it – I trust your judgement, it really depends on the size of your lettuce). Toss through your tofu 'bacon' bits and croutons and serve immediately. Sprinkle with vegan Parmesan if desired.

Caprese Tart

These tarts are so easy to make. Often people make large sheet pan tomato tarts but they can be soggy on the bottom and not as aesthetically pleasing as desired. If you do individual ones, it's instantly a little special, plus it's flaky, puffy, soft and crispy.

MAKES 8 INDIVIDUAL TARTS

2 sheets dairy-free puff pastry
50 g red pesto (page 204)
600 g fresh tomatoes, thinly sliced
100 g Grater Goods Cashew
    Mozzarella, thinly sliced
3 tablespoons soy milk
3 tablespoons olive oil
handful of basil leaves

Preheat oven to 200°C. Defrost pastry and cut into 10 cm squares. Put approx. 1 teaspoon of red pesto into the middle of each square and spread with the back of your spoon. Place one slice of cheese, then 2–3 slices of tomato (depending on the size of your tomatoes) onto each pastry square. Sprinkle with sea salt and black pepper.

Combine soy milk and oil and brush onto the edges of your pastry. Bake for 20–25 minutes until puffed and golden. Top with basil leaves and serve immediately.

When you're entertaining you have to keep things simple; and it is often the simplest things that are the crowd favourites anyway! Easiest option when you have offcuts of puff pastry and zero time up your sleeve...

Pesto Braids
Cut your pastry into long thin strips. Press two strips together at the top. Paint the lengths with red (or green) pesto. Twist the two pieces together (or do three pieces and plait them) until you have a long braid. Bake at 200°C for 20 minutes or until puffy and golden.

White Bean & Garlic Soup

A super simple, super nourishing recipe using just pantry staples. This has been a favourite in our family since Anaïs began eating.

SERVES 2 AS A MAIN / 4 AS AN ENTRÉE

2 tablespoons olive oil
3 cloves garlic, sliced
½ courgette (or squash), sliced
½–1 teaspoon flaky sea salt
1 can white beans (or chickpeas)
½ cup dried pasta (ideally
    something smallish)
1¼ cups water or stock

Gently warm olive oil and garlic on medium heat. Add courgette or any other vege you'd like to add, some sea salt and cook until just starting to soften, about 1 minute.

Add white beans (with most of the liquid from the can), pasta of choice and stock.

Turn up the heat until boiling, then reduce to medium heat for 10–12 minutes, until pasta is just cooked.

Remove ½ cup of soup mixture and blend until creamy. Alternatively, you could use a stick blender to blend part of the soup, or just use a fork to smash some of the beans.

Add blended or smashed beans back into the pan, taste and season with black pepper and salt if needed. Serve topped with olive oil and enjoy with crusty bread.

Roasted Cauliflower & Shallot Socca

Also known as farinata, this chickpea pizza-type thing was my favourite thing to eat on tour. I ate it in thin, crispy slices on the seaside in the Cinque Terre; battered and fried and stuffed into bread as a late night snack in Sicily; and straight out of a portable oven in a marche in the south of France. It can be comfort street food but it can also be a super easy, crowd-pleasing party food or an entrée. It sounds kinda complex but it's actually incredibly easy as soon as you've done it once, and it is 100 per cent worth it. This recipe makes a fairly substantial version of socca. If you want a thinner, crispier version just make this into two 'pizzas' or reduce by a third or a half. Also if you have a small cast iron pan, split the mixture into two. You can do this with the veg, without the veg, with other veg or herbs. Play around with it.

SERVES 4–6

Topping:
2 shallots
¼ cauliflower

Socca:
2 cups chickpea flour
1 tablespoon flaky sea salt
1 tablespoon rosemary, finely
   chopped
a crack of black pepper
1¾ cups cold water
1 tablespoon olive oil
3–4 tablespoons olive oil for cooking

Preheat oven to 200°C. Peel shallots and keep whole. Cut cauliflower into florets. Toss both in olive oil and salt and spread on a baking tray. Bake for 25–30 minutes until cauli is taking some colour and shallots are soft. Remove and set aside.

Heat your oven to its hottest setting, likely 250°C, and allow it to heat while you make the batter.

Add flour, salt, rosemary and pepper to a bowl. Slowly add the water whilst whisking to incorporate. Chickpea flour wants to clump so you have to do this a little carefully. Once combined, add the oil and mix well. Chill in the fridge for 30 minutes.

Place a cast iron pan (any heatproof pan will work but cast iron is best) into the oven. Once the pan is smoking hot, carefully remove from the oven, coat liberally in the rest of your olive oil, pour in the batter and arrange your cauliflower and shallots on top. Place back into the oven and cook for 10 minutes until you can see the edges going golden and the top is firm. If you've reduced the quantities this will be 6–8 minutes.

Remove, sprinkle with extra sea salt and fresh rosemary. Serve hot as squares or pizza slices.

Chickpea 'Tuna' Tartine

We use this chickpea 'tuna' for many things. Eat it as a salad, put it in a wrap for lunchboxes, use as a filling for sushi rolls... it's great. Tartine is simply an open-faced sandwich. It's a great snack, lunch or entrée.

SERVES 4

Chickpea 'Tuna':
1 can chickpeas
12 cm stick of celery, finely diced
¼ cup red pepper, finely diced
1 tablespoon red onion, finely diced
1 tablespoon capers, chopped
2 tablespoons gherkins, diced
   (optional)
3 teaspoons egg-free mayonnaise
1 teaspoon Dijon mustard
zest and juice of ½ lemon
¼ sheet nori, finely cut or blitzed
   into a powder (alternatively you
   could use ½ teaspoon kelp powder)
½ teaspoon dried dill
pinch black pepper
pinch sea salt

To serve:
4 slices toast
8 stalks asparagus or handful of
   microgreens
lemon wedges to serve
capers to garnish (optional)

Drain and rinse chickpeas, place into a bowl and roughly mash with a fork. Add remaining ingredients. Mix well to combine. You can eat this immediately but it's best eaten between 2 and 24 hours after making.

If using asparagus, trim stalks then place in a hot oiled griddle pan. Cook for 5 minutes, turning occasionally.

Toast some slices of sourdough or ciabatta. Top with chickpea mixture, then asparagus or microgreens, squeeze with lemon juice and scatter with extra capers if you like.

Cheesy Savoury Loaf

This will be soft when hot (because of all the melty cheese!) but firm up when cool. Serve hot as an entrée alongside some salad, also makes a great lunchbox item when cold.

SERVES 8

Wet ingredients:
2 tablespoons unsweetened soy
    or coconut yoghurt
½ cup vegetable oil, plus extra
    to grease
1 cup soy milk
1 tablespoon ground flaxseed

150 g dairy-free cheddar, coarsely
    grated plus extra for scattering
    (don't be stingy!)
¼ cup roasted red peppers, chopped
¼ cup sundried tomatoes
    in oil, chopped (you could use
    the oil for the vegetable oil)
1 spring onion, finely sliced
2 cups plain gluten-free flour
1 tablespoon baking powder
1 teaspoon baking soda
2 teaspoons nutritional yeast
½ teaspoon flaky sea salt
½ teaspoon dried dill or dried herbs
¼ teaspoon white pepper
½ teaspoon onion powder (optional)
¼ teaspoon garlic powder (optional)
1 cup green leaves (spinach, kale,
    beet tops)

Preheat oven to 180°C. Grease and line the base and sides of a 12 x 24 cm loaf pan with baking paper.

Combine wet ingredients and sit for 2 minutes so the flaxseed can soften and swell slightly. Add remaining ingredients and mix well to combine. Mixture will thicken as it's mixed. Spoon into prepared loaf pan and bake for 45 minutes or until cooked through when tested with a skewer. Cool in pan for 10 minutes then cut and serve.

Loaf can be stored in a sealed container in the fridge for 1 week.

Omelette

We created an omelette recipe yonks ago but lost it! We really sucked at systems and paperwork back then. Thankfully our dear Maki is brilliant – I simply gave a her a list of the things I remembered being in it and she came up with a recipe. We did a few staff taste tests and finally came to this version. Loads of people just use chickpea flour but a tofu version is softer and creamier, closer to a fluffy French-style omelette. You'll need a non-stick frying pan!

MAKES 2 OMELETTES

2 tablespoons olive oil
¼ cup dairy-free cheddar, coarsely
   grated
¼ red pepper, finely diced

Omelette batter:
250 g firm tofu, drained
¼ cup chickpea flour
1 cup soy milk (or any
   plant milk)
1 tablespoon nutritional yeast
1 teaspoon baking powder
½ teaspoon black salt
½ teaspoon garlic powder (optional)
½ teaspoon ground turmeric

For the batter place all ingredients in a blender or food processor and blend until you have a smooth batter.

Heat 1 tablespoon of oil in a roughly 25 cm non-stick frying pan over a medium-low heat. Add 1 cup (250 ml) of the batter and tilt to spread across the pan. Cook, without touching, for 4–5 minutes or until you see bubbles start to appear across the entire omelette and middle is puffing up slightly.

Sprinkle over half the cheese and increase heat to medium-high. Use a spatula to shimmy the edge then fold over to create a half moon. Cook for a further 1–2 minutes or until cheese is melted and oozing out the sides.

Slide onto a plate and repeat with remaining oil, batter and cheese. Serve scattered with red pepper, herbs of your choice, chilli flakes or cracked pepper – whatever you like.

Artwork by Shaun McCarroll

04/
/Mains

/ Here we have the mains. Mostly because they're slightly more constructed than the other recipes. Truly, when you're liberated from the idea of basing all meals around a source of protein, anything can be entrée, anything can be main. My favourite way to entertain is to create two things from apéro, two things from entrée, something from mains and something from dessert, put it all out on a large table and call 'à table!' /

Smoky Spanish Beans

¼ cup olive oil
2 onions, roughly chopped
½ red pepper, roughly chopped
100 g vegan chorizo, chopped
    (optional)
2 teaspoons smoked paprika
½ teaspoon dried oregano
1 tablespoon tomato paste
2 cans butter beans (cannellini beans
    also work)
1 can of water or vegetable stock
fresh chillies to serve

Add oil to a heavy-based pan on a medium heat. Add onions and red pepper, some salt and pepper, and cook until softening and brown. Add chorizo if using.

Once everything is starting to stick, add paprika, oregano and tomato paste and cook for a minute until fragrant. Add the beans – one can drained, one can with the liquid. Add can of water or vegetable stock.

Cook gently for 25 minutes until thick and rich. Serve with crusty bread, fresh chillies and your favourite steamed greens.

Creamy Mushroom Pasta

You won't believe how creamy and awesome this is. Using sunflower seeds to make cream sounds like a disgusting-yet-healthy hack. It's not. I mean, it is healthy. It just also happens to be frickin' delicious, super decadent and really easy.

SERVES 2-3

180 g dried pasta of your choice
¼ cup olive oil
200 g mixed mushrooms, sliced
1 small onion, finely sliced
2 cloves garlic, finely sliced
pinch salt and pepper
handful of fresh thyme
1 cup sunflower cream (page 208)

Cook pasta as per packet instructions. Drain, reserving ¼ cup cooking liquid (for the love of starch, don't rinse your pasta!).

Heat olive oil in a frying pan until medium-hot. Add mushrooms, onion and garlic, salt and pepper and fresh thyme leaves.

Once your mushrooms have some colour on them, add sunflower cream to the frying pan along with ¼ cup of pasta water. Cook for 3–4 minutes. Taste and adjust seasoning.

Toss through the drained pasta and serve with plenty of black pepper and more fresh thyme leaves.

Tofu En Papillote

En papillote simply means cooked in a paper pouch. I've had tofu fish many times but I was craving something like a steamed fish so I decided to try it en papillote. It's really good and really fun. You can do this in one big paper pocket or individual pockets so you can serve it in its paper and let guests or family members tear it open.

SERVES 2

Tofu 'steaks':
300 g firm tofu
½ sheet nori
½ bulb fennel
2 thick slices lemon
1 teaspoon fresh thyme or
   dill, finely chopped

Marinade:
¼ cup white wine
juice of ½ lemon
2 tablespoons olive oil
⅛ teaspoon dried herbs
   de Provence (or mixed herbs)
⅛ teaspoon dried dill
pinch white pepper
cracked black pepper
½ teaspoon flaky sea salt

Cut tofu through the middle to create two 3–4 cm thick steaks. Drain on a tea towel while preparing marinade. Combine all marinade ingredients in a bowl and whisk to combine.

Score tofu on one side, carefully cutting to the middle of the tofu, without cutting right through. Make each slice a couple of millimetres apart so you get a 'gill' vibe. Place tofu into a shallow dish and pour the marinade over the steaks. Cover and leave to rest in a fridge for at least an hour, preferably overnight.

Reserving the marinade, remove steaks from marinade and place onto nori sheet, un-scored side down. Cut around the steaks and discard any excess nori sheet, reserving it to throw into stocks, soups or carrot lox (page 48). Your tofu will stick to the seaweed, creating a nori 'skin' on one side of the tofu steak.

Slice fennel bulb into thick slices and set aside. Take a long length of recycled baking paper, fold in half, then fold both sides 3 times to create a papillote or paper pocket. You will need to make two. You can tie or staple these if you like but they'll hold pretty well with 3 folds.

Heat a little oil in a pan on medium heat until almost smoking. Carefully place each steak into the pan, scored side down. Fry for 2–3 minutes without touching, until a slight skin forms on the tofu. Place the tofu steaks into each papillote with the equally divided fennel, lemon slices and herbs. Pour the marinade over and roll the open edge downwards to seal the pocket.

Bake in a preheated oven at 200°C for 20–25 minutes. Serve your steaks and fennel pieces with a creamy sauce or the leftover marinade, some green beans, potatoes, and of course... crusty bread.

Moroccan Baked Aubergine

SERVES 2

10 cherry tomatoes
⅓ cup Amazigh harissa* (page 212)
1 aubergine
½ cup 'yoghurt' sauce**
   (page 206)

To garnish:
2 teaspoons toasted pine nuts
½ teaspoon toasted cumin seeds
bunch fresh coriander
bunch fresh mint

*Harissa could be substituted with
store-bought harissa but it's worth
making this epic sauce if you can be
bothered!*

**‘Yoghurt’ sauce could be substituted
by adding some salt and lemon juice to
an unsweetened dairy-free yoghurt of
your choice.*

Place cherry tomatoes (and chillies, if making harissa) into an
oven preheated to 200°C. Sprinkle with a little salt and olive
oil and roast for 25 minutes until soft and taking some colour.

Remove tomatoes and set aside. Place chillies into a mortar
and pestle or blender and follow harissa recipe.

Cut aubergine into 2 halves lengthwise. Score diagonally
with a sharp knife and spread harissa across each surface,
reserving some for serving. Roast aubergine halves (in
the lower half of your oven) for 40–45 minutes, until soft.
Remove from the oven, spread with a little reserved fresh
harissa, drizzle with 'yoghurt' sauce and top with toasted
pine nuts, cumin seeds and fresh herbs.

Garlic & Herb 'Pork' Sausage

This is a simple seitan sausage that I make for general purpose. It's great in the cassoulet (page 128) and creamy polenta (page 142).

MAKES 4 SAUSAGES

2 large cloves garlic
2 tablespoons sunflower oil

Wet:
1 can cannellini beans with liquid
  (400 g)
½ cup warm water
1 teaspoon liquid smoke or smoked
  paprika
1 teaspoon vegan chicken stock
  powder
1 teaspoon vegan beef stock powder
1 teaspoon sugar
1 teaspoon soy sauce
2 tablespoons sunflower oil
½ teaspoon balsamic vinegar

Dry:
1½ cups gluten flour
¼ cup wheat flour
¼ cup nutritional yeast
3 teaspoons onion powder
5 teaspoons garlic powder
½ teaspoon ground allspice
scant ¼ teaspoon black pepper
2 tablespoons mushroom powder*
2 teaspoons salt
1 tablespoon + 1 teaspoon dried
  marjoram

**finely ground, dried shiitake
mushrooms*

Finely chop garlic cloves and add to a cold pan with oil. Heat gently until fragrant, be careful not to let it brown. Take off heat and set aside.

Add wet ingredients to a blender or mixer and blend well.

Combine blended mixture and cooked garlic with dry ingredients. Knead for 3 minutes. Add more flour if mixture is too wet to handle. Wrap into 200 g sausages and steam for 40 minutes.

At home people commonly use baking paper, then tinfoil for their wrap. You can also use a silicone mould or cloth to form your sausage but make sure it's wrapped tightly, as it will expand while cooking.

Chill overnight. Keep in a sealed container for up to 10 days. Best sliced or diced and fried, or fried whole as a breakfast sausage.

Comforting, creamy, hearty cassoulet. Using great sausage and bouillon/stock is key here. No roux or wine needed, just a simple classic to comfort you on cold evenings.

White Bean & Garlic Sausage Cassoulet

SERVES 4

2 tablespoons olive oil
1 medium onion
200 g garlic and herb 'pork' sausage
  (page 124) or Grater Goods Kielbasa
2 medium waxy potatoes
1 can cannellini beans
1¼ cups vegetable stock or
  vegan chicken stock
parsley or thyme to serve

Peel and dice onion. Dice sausage and potatoes into bite-sized chunks. Add olive oil to a heavy-based pan and heat to medium heat. Add onion and sauté for a couple of minutes until softening. Add sausage and fry off until browning slightly. Add beans (with liquid), stock and potatoes and stir.

Reduce to low, cover and leave to simmer for 25–30 minutes until potatoes are cooked through but holding their shape and sauce is thick. Check often and add a little extra stock if needed.

Toss through some herbs before serving with crusty bread and your favourite steamed greens.

Beet Bourguignon

SERVES 4

3 tablespoons olive oil
1 onion, finely chopped
1 carrot, chopped into 1 cm pieces
400 g beetroot, cut into 3 cm batons
2 cloves of garlic, finely chopped
2 sprigs thyme, leaves picked
½ teaspoon onion powder
⅓ cup pinot noir
1 tablespoon tamari or light
  soy sauce
2 cups vegetable stock
salt and pepper to taste
200 g mushrooms, halved
1 tablespoon cornstarch

Heat 2 tablespoons of oil in a heavy-based saucepan over medium-high heat. Add onion and cook, stirring, for 3 minutes or until softened. Add carrot and beetroot pieces and cook, stirring, for 5 minutes or until beetroot is slightly tender.

Add garlic, thyme sprigs and onion powder and cook until aromatic. Increase heat to high and add the wine, bring mixture to the boil and cook for 2 minutes or until reduced slightly. Add soy sauce and stock and return to a simmer. Reduce heat to low, cover with a lid and cook, removing lid halfway, for 40 minutes or until beetroot is cooked through and tender. Season to taste.

Meanwhile, drizzle remaining tablespoon of oil into a frying pan. Add the mushrooms, cut side down, and place over high heat. Cook, without touching, for 4 minutes or until golden on one side. Remove from heat and stand until required.

When the stew is cooked, combine cornstarch with 2 tablespoons of the stew liquid to dissolve. Add mixture to stew along with the cooked mushrooms. Stir to combine and cook for a further 2 minutes or until thickened and glossy.

Serve with crusty bread, a sprinkling of fresh thyme and plenty of fresh black pepper.

MAKING DOUGH FOR SPINACH RAVIOLI,
RECIPE NEXT PAGE.

 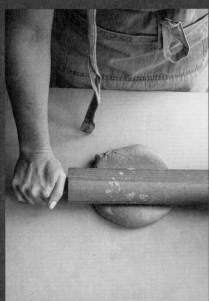 

Spinach Ravioli with Cashew Ricotta

This is a good dinner party option but I dare ya to make it when eating alone. There is no more satisfying self care than taking the time to cook and plate something fussy just for yourself. Cheat this by using store-bought dumpling wrappers instead of making the dough from scratch. Use up any leftover dough or wrap and freeze for another day.

MAKES APPROX. 10 RAVIOLI

¾ cup wheat flour*
½ teaspoon sea salt
¼ cup water
50 g spinach (or chard or parsley)
1 tablespoon olive oil
50 g cashew ricotta (page 22)
basil or thyme leaves to garnish

*You can use a bourgeois flour for this if you want but all-purpose flour will work just fine.

Place flour into a bowl with salt. Blend water, spinach leaves and oil in a bullet or high-speed blender. Add to flour and bring together with your hands, adding a touch of water or flour if needed. Knead dough for a few minutes until you have a smooth-ish round ball of green dough. Wrap and rest for 60 minutes.

Roll out your dough until 1 mm thick. Cut into rounds approximately 7–8 cm across. Place 1 teaspoon cashew ricotta into the centre of one round. Use your fingertip to spread a little water around the edge of the circle and place another round on top, carefully pressing the air out and sealing the edge. Repeat for all ravioli.

Place one raviolo at a time into salted boiling water. Cook for 2–3 minutes until al dente (depending on thickness of your dough). Remove with slotted spoon and serve atop a rich tomato sauce (page 200), scattered with pepper, olive oil and fresh herbs.

Creamy Polenta with Lentils & Sausage

A hearty, comfort food for winter meals. It's insanely delicious and worth getting acquainted with polenta for, if you're not already.

SERVES 4

2 cups vegetable stock

2½ cups soy or oat milk (plus extra on standby)

1 cup medium grind polenta

1 teaspoon flaky sea salt

3 tablespoons vegan butter or dairy-free margarine

1 tablespoon vegan Parmesan (optional)

1 cup cooked Puy green lentils (use preparation from page 74)

2 vegetarian sausages (or 1 Grater Goods Kielbasa, or one 'pork' sausage from page 124), fried and sliced

4 sprigs fresh thyme

Bring stock and milk to the boil. Slowly pour polenta in, whisking, until all polenta is in and there are no lumps. Add salt.

Turn the heat down to low, cover and leave to cook, checking and stirring regularly with a wooden spoon. You want the polenta to lose its grittiness and become smooth. This will take around 30 minutes but it depends on the polenta so keep an eye on it. If it gets too thick, just add a touch of water or milk. You may also need to add some milk to loosen just before serving.

Once cooked, remove from the heat, add butter (and Parmesan if using) and stir through.

Divide onto plates and top with lentils and sausage slices. Serve immediately with a sprinkle of black pepper and fresh thyme.

Green Beans with Thyme & Walnut

Yes, I'm sneaking some sides in here. Who can be bothered with a sides chapter? Plus, I could eat this entire thing as my dinner. Come at me.

SERVES 6 AS A SIDE

400 g green beans, ends trimmed off
2 tablespoons cashew Parmesan
  (page 202)
1 clove garlic, thinly sliced
zest and juice of ½ lemon
1 sprig thyme
½ cup walnuts, roughly chopped
salt and black pepper to taste
2 tablespoons olive oil

Preheat the oven to 180°C. Blanch your beautiful green beans for 4 minutes in salted water, drain and arrange on an oven tray. Combine Parmesan, garlic, lemon zest, thyme leaves and chopped walnuts and scatter evenly onto the beans.

Add some salt and freshly ground black pepper. Drizzle over the olive oil, ensuring it coats the beans evenly. Bake for 8–10 minutes until tender.

Squeeze over the lemon juice and serve.

Cauliflower Dauphinoise

Gratin or dauphinoise is traditionally a super rich dish of layered potatoes with cream and sometimes cheese. This version is made entirely of cauliflower and potato but it's rich and creamy, with a crunchy, crispy top. And look, I'm not saying you should use this dish to trick family and friends into eating more vegetables... but if they just happen to eat extra vegetables whilst you're feeding them delicious food, where's the harm?

SERVES 6

cauliflower cream (page 208)
⅓ cup soy cream (or plant milk such
   as soy or oat)
5 medium to large starchy potatoes
¼–⅓ cup vegan butter or dairy-free
   margarine
pinch nutmeg (optional)

Prepare cauliflower cream as per recipe. Add cream or milk and stir to combine. Adjust seasoning if needed – you'll need to make sure there is plenty of salt in this because potatoes love salt.

Preheat your oven to 180°C. Slice the potatoes very thinly using a mandolin or speed peeler (or cut as thinly as you can with a sharp knife). Place potato slices and cream into a large bowl and combine gently with your hands until all potato slices are well coated.

Layer your potatoes in a greased oven dish. Top with any leftover cream, some black pepper and a pinch of nutmeg (optional). Then dot with little scoops or cubes of vegan butter all over. Cover with a lid or foil and bake for 1 hour 15 minutes. Remove the lid and bake for a further 10 minutes. If you want a slightly browned top you may like to switch to grill for a further 5 minutes. Serve hot as a side dish.

Simple 'Super' Greens

This sounds too simple to be delicious but it's so good! Green leaves are essential for everyone's health and if you prepare them correctly, that is NOT a punishment.

SERVES 6 AS A SIDE

300 g dark greens (kale, chard, spinach, beet tops)
2 tablespoons olive oil
4 cloves garlic, finely chopped
1 small onion, finely chopped
1 teaspoon salt
black pepper to taste
1 tablespoon sliced almonds

De-stem your greens if needed. Chop roughly.

Heat a frying pan gently with oil, garlic and onion. Once warm, add leaves, salt and pepper and cook on a low heat, moving as needed. Let them wilt a little and kind of cook in their own juices. I like them with some bite still but you can take them as far as you want – just don't add any water! Taste and add salt if needed.

Meanwhile toast almonds.

Arrange greens on a platter once cooked to your liking. Top with toasted almond slices or another toasted nut or seed.

Open Hours
10am - Late
Tues - Sun

05/
/Desserts

/ Sugar is Youssef's love language. As parents we're by no means anti-sugar but we believe sugar should be part of something wonderful – not solidified into garbage food like candy. It should be used to achieve deliciousness. A perfect bite of tart. A refreshing lick of a fresh sorbet. We appreciate balance – grissini covered in dark chocolate, cookies sprinkled with sea salt ... obviously you can reduce or increase the sweetness of these recipes to your taste and above all else – enjoy food, enjoy life. /

MAKING CRÊPES,
RECIPE NEXT PAGE.

Crêpes

A classic family favourite by Youssef – he and Anaïs love to make crêpes together. This will seem thinner than most pancake recipes, because you want a nice thin crêpe. Omit the sugar and vanilla extract and switch to buckwheat flour for savoury crêpes.

MAKES APPROX. 10

150 g dairy-free butter or margarine
1 teaspoon vanilla extract
1 tablespoon raw sugar
pinch salt
350 g plain flour
400 ml soy milk
300 ml water

Melt butter or margarine and place into a bowl. Add vanilla, sugar and salt and mix well until incorporated.

Place flour into another bowl, make a well and pour in the melted butter mixture, ¾ of the milk and ¼ of the water. Mix well until you have a batter with no lumps. Add remaining liquid until the right consistency.

Leave to rest for 20 minutes in the fridge. Pour a ladle-full into a non-stick frying pan (or crêpe maker) with a little butter or oil. Cook until bubbling, flip and cook until lightly browned on both sides. Eat right away with toppings of your choice.

Tiramisu

SERVES 2

3 madeleines* (page 170)
110 ml strong coffee
½ cup dairy-free mascarpone
    (page 214)
dark chocolate or cocoa powder
    to finish

*An alternative to madeleines would
be vegan sponge or store-bought
vegan sponge fingers.*

Once you have mascarpone and madeleines made, this is the
easiest thing in the world to put together – even if you've had
a few wines with dinner!

Find a couple of beautiful glasses. Tear the madeleines up into
rough pieces and layer with coffee and mascarpone twice.

Top with shaved chocolate or dusted cocoa powder and an
offcut of puff pastry from the mille feuille recipe (page 186)
cooked between 2 pans.

Frangipane

Maki made this incredible creation. A customer favourite – rich, with a beautiful bite.

SERVES 12

Crust:
225 g oat flour
175 g almond flour
3 tablespoons maple syrup
1½ teaspoons dairy-free margarine
45 g coconut oil (melted)
pinch salt

Filling:
190 g almond flour
60 g oat flour
1½ tablespoons cornstarch
1½ teaspoons baking powder
130 g sugar
130 g dairy-free margarine
1 teaspoon vanilla extract
4½ tablespoons dairy-free milk
   (such as soy)

Preheat oven to 160°C. Combine crust ingredients and mix well. Press firmly into a greased 25 cm pie dish.

For the filling, combine almond flour, oat flour, cornstarch and baking powder in a bowl. In another bowl, beat the sugar and margarine together until creamed. Add sugar and margarine mix to flour mix, add vanilla and milk. Combine everything well. Pour into the crust. Bake for 60–70 minutes.

Drizzle with a bit of extra maple syrup (optional). Allow to cool before serving.

Best served with a dollop of mascarpone (page 214) or coconut yoghurt.

Madeleines

Max makes our 'meats' and 'cheeses'. He's super kind and clever... and a French pastry chef. He created this gorgeous recipe and makes several versions so feel free to play around with the flavour profile. Lemon zest is a super nice addition.

MAKES 25

1 cup almond flour
⅔ cup raw sugar
1 tablespoon baking powder
1¼ cups wheat flour
1 cup plant milk (soy or oat)
½ cup oil (sunflower, rice bran or coconut)
1 teaspoon vanilla extract

Preheat the oven to 220°C. In a bowl mix all dry ingredients together. In a separate bowl mix milk and oil together and add to the dry mix. Add vanilla extract.

When well mixed, pour into the madeleine tray. Bake for 5 minutes at 220°C then reduce the temperature to 170°C and bake for a further 5 minutes until golden.

Fudgy Brownies

Chef Max has created this rich, delicious fudgy treat which is incredibly popular with our customers. Here at Grater Goods we feel strongly that brownies <u>have</u> to be fudgy – cakey brownies can 'get in a bin' – or go be cake.

MAKES ONE LARGE SHEET TRAY

2 flax eggs (6 tablespoons water mixed with 2 tablespoons ground flaxseed)
¾ cup raw sugar/coconut sugar
½ cup coconut oil (melted)
¼ cup warm water
1 teaspoon vanilla extract
¾ cup cocoa powder
1 cup almond flour
½ teaspoon sea salt
¼ teaspoon baking soda
⅓ cup freeze-dried raspberries
¼ cup dark choc chips

Top:
⅓ cup dark choc chips
1 tablespoon freeze-dried raspberries

Preheat oven to 160°C. In a large bowl add flax eggs, raw sugar and coconut oil, mix until combined. Add water and vanilla extract. Add cocoa powder, almond flour, sea salt and baking soda and mix. Add the raspberries or any other flavours you wish. Combine, until fully incorporated. Stir in choc chips.

Pour into a greased pan and bake for 35 minutes.

As soon as it comes out of the oven add the second measure of choc chips on top of the hot brownie to melt it, and spread it over the surface. Then sprinkle the raspberries over the top and cool completely.

You can top with anything you like if you don't have freeze-dried fruit – melted chocolate, cocoa powder, walnuts…

Crème Brûlée

1 cup oat milk
1 can coconut milk (400 ml)
3 tablespoons caster sugar
1 tablespoon vanilla paste (or seeds
   of one vanilla pod)
¼ cup cornflour
caster sugar to finish

A note about sugar:
If you're avoiding all animal products,
some sugars are processed using
animal products. Chelsea sugar in
New Zealand is all vegan, but if you're
elsewhere you may want to research
which sugars use animal products and
which don't.

Add oat milk, coconut milk, sugar, vanilla and cornflour to a cold pan. Whisk together and warm, stirring, until thickened. Pour into ramekins and leave to set in the fridge for between 2 and 24 hours.

These can be eaten as is, like a creamy decadent pudding, but if you have a blow torch all humans love breaking through that crunchy sugary top, so it's worth the effort of going full brûlée. Sprinkle the tops of your puddings with caster sugar and run a blow torch over the top until it browns and then hardens.

Lemon Tart

Created by one of our brilliant chefs, Annika, this is truly one of my favourite sweet things now. It's sweet and also sour, crunchy and soft. Such a great recipe.

SERVES 12

Sweet tart base:
100 g almond flour
100 g raw sugar
80 g crushed almonds
pinch salt
50 g vegan butter or margarine

Lemon curd filling:
1 can coconut cream (400 ml)
zest of 2 lemons
1 cup freshly squeezed lemon juice
pinch salt
½–1 cup raw sugar
⅓ cup cornflour

Preheat oven to 160°C. For the tart base, mix dry ingredients together. Melt butter and add into dry mix. Combine well. Press into a 25 cm fluted tart pan evenly with tart base going about 1 cm up on the edges of the tin. Bake for 15–20 minutes or until golden brown.

Remove from oven and allow to cool.

For the filling, place coconut cream, zest of one lemon, juice, salt and ½ cup of raw sugar into a pot. Mix with a whisk, taste. If you want it sweeter, add more sugar.

Add the cornflour and whisk to dissolve. After a couple of minutes, you will notice the curd getting thicker, let it heat up for a minute more (whisking all the time!). Then take off the heat and pour on top of the tart base immediately as the curd sets very fast. Chill in the fridge for at least an hour.

Sprinkle some extra lemon zest on top for an extra zesty kick (optional), serve with whipped coconut cream and/or fresh fruits/berries.

MAKING MILLE FEUILLE,
RECIPE NEXT PAGE.

Mille Feuille

Youssef is awesome at fiddly things. His attention to detail and patience is amazing and makes him great at things like this delicious dessert. Although it looks tricky, it's a surprisingly simple hack. You can cook the pastry in a pan, on a flat grill or even in a toasted sandwich maker/grill press.

SERVES 4

2 sheets dairy-free puff pastry
½ cup mascarpone (page 214) or
    whipped plant-based cream
½ cup hazelnuts or berries
icing sugar to finish

Cut pastry into 6 x 12 cm rectangles.

Place your mascarpone into a piping bag (or a plastic bag with a corner cut out).

Cook pastry sheets in a dry pan with another heavy pan on top, to prevent puffing. Cook at medium heat until brown.

Layer your pastry sheets with mascarpone dollops or swirls, hazelnuts or berries and another pastry layer until you've created a beautiful, layered dessert. Top with icing sugar.

The easiest chocolate sauce hack:
All you need is hot chocolate powder and water or milk – make into a paste and add a little liquid at a time until you have a sauce.

Spiced Poached Pears

SERVES 4

4 firm pears (I used Beurre Bosc)
500 ml water
200 g caster sugar
4 tablespoons fresh ginger, finely
  grated
1 teaspoon vanilla extract
2 star anise (optional)
juice of ½ lemon
2 tablespoons slivered almonds,
  toasted

Put the water, sugar, ginger, vanilla extract and star anise into a large pan and bring to the boil. Turn down the heat and simmer for 5 minutes, or until the sugar has dissolved.

Meanwhile peel the pears, then cut in half lengthways and core. Coat in the lemon juice to stop them from going brown.

Transfer the pears to the pan containing the syrup, ensuring the liquid covers the pears. Bring to the boil.

Reduce the heat and simmer for 25–30 minutes, until the pears are just tender. Leave them to cool slightly in the syrup.

Serve warm with chocolate ginger ice cream (page 190) and sprinkled with almonds.

Chocolate Ginger Ice Cream

SERVES 6

200 g pitted dates
60 ml almond milk
1 can coconut cream (400 ml),
  chilled overnight in the fridge
2 tablespoons cocoa powder
½ teaspoon vanilla extract
25 g crystallised ginger, chopped into
  small pieces
¼ cup slivered almonds, toasted
generous pinch salt flakes

Soak dates in boiling water for 10 minutes then drain. Place into a bullet blender or food processor with the almond milk and blend, so you get a thick paste.

Empty the chilled coconut cream into a large mixing bowl, and using an electric whisk, whip until creamy and smooth. Add the cocoa powder, vanilla and date paste and mix until fully combined.

Gently fold in the crystallised ginger and almonds and transfer to a freezer-safe container. Sprinkle the sea salt on top, cover and place in the freezer overnight.

Remove from freezer 30 minutes prior to serving.

This ice cream will keep in the freezer for a few weeks, but will go icy in time, so it is best eaten within a week.

06/
/Basics

/ You won't believe how many things are creamy, aside from cream. We use white beans, cauliflower, sunflower seeds, cashews, tahini and more to bring delicious, creamy unctuousness to the table. The accidental benefit is that these recipes are WAY healthier than traditional versions. I've been plant-based for so long now I forget that these basics aren't everyone's basics. So here are a few simple classics that I'd like to share with you. These can be used in the recipes in this book or used across your repertoire. Some of these come from the school of 'anything you can do, I can do vegan'. Others are traditionally plant-based things with our twists. /

Creamy Cashew Dressing

½ cup soaked cashews*
½ cup water
½ clove garlic (or 1 teaspoon
   garlic powder)
½ teaspoon sugar
1 teaspoon Dijon mustard
1 tablespoon olive oil
2 teaspoons nutritional yeast
1 teaspoon sea salt
2 tablespoons white wine vinegar
1 good pinch freshly ground
   black pepper

*Best if soaked overnight but if you're
disorganised (like me) simply pour
boiling water over raw nuts and leave
for at least 10 minutes before blending.*

Blend all ingredients together until very smooth. Taste and adjust seasoning if needed.

Tahini Dressing

3 tablespoons tahini
2–3 teaspoons lemon juice
6–7 tablespoons water
¼ –½ teaspoon salt
pinch black pepper (optional)
½ clove garlic

This is an approximate recipe as it depends on the type of tahini you use so trust your instincts here!

Add tahini to a small bowl. Add the lemon juice and water, 1 tablespoon at a time, stirring to combine. This will seize up and then soften as you add more liquid. Stop adding water when you have a creamy, drizzle-able consistency. Add salt, pepper and finely grated or crushed garlic.

Taste and adjust as desired.

Egg-Free Aioli

Maki has created this fantastic aioli. Completely egg-free, with a perfect balance. It's addictive and super easy to make. You can try using other plant milks but the protein levels in soy milk makes for the best results in my experience. This is a generous amount, but trust me when I say it's incredibly moreish.

MAKES 1 TUB

500 ml soy milk
3 cups sunflower oil
1 tablespoon Dijon mustard
1½ teaspoons wholegrain mustard
1 tablespoon sea salt
3 cloves garlic
50 ml white wine vinegar

Combine soy milk, oil and mustard and using a stick blender, blend until it emulsifies and goes thick and awesome. Add all remaining ingredients and blend until well combined.

Rich Tomato Sauce

This is my go-to at home. It's simple, everyone loves it and it works with everything. Spoon it over spaghetti, smear it under grilled vegetables, spread it over a pizza base. If I'm making it for Anaïs I'll finely grate courgette and red pepper in before adding tomatoes.

MAKES 1½ CUPS

4 tablespoons olive oil
8–10 capers
½ teaspoon mixed dried herbs
1 can whole organic tomatoes
1 teaspoon flaky sea salt
pinch black pepper

Warm oil in a pan. Add capers and herbs and cook for 1 minute. Add tomatoes, salt and pepper. Stir to break up the tomatoes slightly and combine ingredients. Simmer for 20 minutes uncovered; you need to be okay with it spitting tomato all over your kitchen.

Remove from heat. If cooking causally, grab a potato masher or fork and smash the tomatoes to make a rough sauce. If you'd prefer a smooth sauce, blend until smooth. Check seasoning and adjust if needed.

Cashew Parmesan

MAKES 1 CUP

1 cup raw cashews (unsoaked)
2 tablespoons nutritional yeast
2 teaspoons lemon juice
1 teaspoon sea salt
1 teaspoon miso paste
½ teaspoon garlic powder

Place all ingredients into a blender or food processor and pulse until you have a coarse powder. Spread onto a tray and bake in a preheated oven at 180°C for 8–10 minutes to dry it out. Test and adjust seasoning if needed. It may need some extra salt at this stage so trust your tastebuds.

Keep in a sealed container in the fridge for up to 10 days and sprinkle over your dishes.

This is awesome sprinkled on avocado toast or tossed through pasta. You can also add it to pestos.

Red Pesto

MAKES 1 LARGE JAR

300 g sundried tomatoes
140 g pumpkin seeds
1 teaspoon salt
pinch black pepper
20 g fresh garlic
200 g sunflower oil
5 ml lemon juice

Blend all ingredients together. Taste and adjust if needed. Store in a jar in the fridge for up to 2 weeks and top up with oil when needed.

Use as a spread, dip, pasta sauce or throw into soups and stews for an umami hit. A firm family favourite (right) is to cook up some spaghetti, stir in a generous dollop of pesto and sprinkle with Parmesan. So simple, so good.

'Yoghurt' Sauce

Full disclosure – this 'yoghurt' sauce contains no yoghurt. You can totally use yoghurt if you want but there's a special funky flavour in this sauce that I love, plus it's a great hack if you either can't find a dairy-free yoghurt that is sour enough (relatable!) or don't have any yoghurt in the house but have an old jar of sauerkraut in the back of your fridge (also relatable).

MAKES APPROX. 1½ CUPS

1 block tofu (300 g)
½ cup sauerkraut
1 teaspoon flaky sea salt
¾ cup water
1 teaspoon lemon juice
1 small clove garlic

Add all ingredients to a blender. Taste, adjust salt if needed as the seasoning will depend on the sauerkraut you use. As a general rule, add salt until you exclaim 'yum'!

Cauliflower Cream

MAKES 1–2 CUPS (DEPENDING ON THE SIZE OF YOUR CAULI)

4 cloves garlic
1 shallot or small onion
1 medium head cauliflower
½ cup plant milk (oat or soy work
    well. You may need a little extra
    depending on size of cauli)
2 tablespoons dairy-free butter
1 teaspoon flaky sea salt
black pepper to taste
pinch nutmeg

Peel garlic and onion. Leave garlic whole, slice onion. Roughly chop cauliflower into chunks.

Add all ingredients to a large pot and bring to the boil. Reduce heat, cover and simmer for 10 minutes until cauli is soft. Transfer to a blender and blend until smooth and luscious. Taste and season if needed.

Sunflower Cream

MAKE 1½ CUPS

½ cup sunflower seeds
¾ cup water
1 teaspoon salt
¼ teaspoon freshly ground black
    pepper

Place sunflower seeds into a bowl, pour boiling water over them and leave to soak for 2 hours (alternatively boil them for 5 minutes). Drain and rinse.

Place soaked sunflower seeds, water, salt and pepper into a high-speed blender or bullet and blend until smooth and creamy. Use as a cream in pasta dishes, soups and salads.

Amazigh Harissa

We love harissa but haven't found a shop-bought one in Aotearoa that we love. It's also tricky to find good dried chillies here, so I developed this chilli pesto with things that I could easily source, inspired by traditional Moroccan flavours, as a love letter to Youssef's heritage. We use the term Amazigh in place of Berber and recommend you do the same.

MAKES 1 SMALL JAR

6 fresh cayenne chillies (those long, red, juicy chillies found commonly in supermarkets)
2 teaspoons cumin seeds
1 teaspoon sea salt
4 cloves garlic
1 teaspoon sugar
2 tablespoons tomato paste
2 teaspoons white vinegar
150 ml olive oil

Preheat oven to 200°C. Place chillies onto a tray, drizzle with a little oil and sprinkle with a little salt. Bake for 25–30 minutes until starting to blacken slightly.

Toast cumin seeds gently in a small pan until fragrant, then smash them up in a mortar and pestle with salt. If using a blender, just throw them in with everything else.

Remove the green stalks of chillies and throw whole chillies into your mortar and pestle or blender. When using these chillies, I highly recommend throwing these in whole, with skin and seeds for heat and char but if you're sensitive to spice or texture, remove the seeds and skin.

Add all other ingredients to mortar (or blender) and smash until you have a pesto.

Keep in a jar in the fridge for as long as you want, topping up with oil as needed.

Mascarpone

This recipe is unbelievable. It truly has to be tried. It's creamy, thick and sweet, but not too sweet. It's just amazing. Enjoy it on the side of cake, with berries, in the tiramisu (page 166) or mille feuille (page 186).

MAKES 1 MEDIUM SIZE BOWL

300 g tofu
1 tablespoon cider vinegar
2 tablespoons lemon juice
⅓ cup icing sugar
1½ teaspoons xanthan gum
1 tablespoon vanilla paste (or 1½
   teaspoons vanilla extract)
1½ teaspoons flaky sea salt
6 tablespoons melted coconut oil

Add all ingredients to a blender and blend until very smooth. Chill overnight, mix again thoroughly and serve.

Apple Jam

Here is one of Annika's delicious recipes. This can be used as a filling in her tart base or used just as a condiment for brunch or apéro.

MAKES 1 MEDIUM JAR

500 g red apples
200 g brown sugar
2 cinnamon sticks
water

Chop red apples into small pieces, there is no need to peel. Put into a pot with sugar and cinnamon sticks. Cover with water.

Simmer on medium heat until almost all the water has reduced, and jam is golden and caramelised – this will take a couple of hours. If jam is not ready before all the water has boiled off, add a little bit more water and continue simmering. Remove cinnamon sticks when jam is ready.

Store and use as a jam or as a tart filling.

Recipe index

Thank you

I really hope you all enjoy this book and get some inspo, good meals and great times from it. This book was a passion project – we're so excited about great food and about showing ya'll what's possible with plants.

I want to say an enormous thank you to Tonia for pulling this book together, for her incredible talents, patience and encouragement.

Thank you to all the recipe contributors – I'm privileged to work with you all and incredibly inspired by you. Massive thanks to the whole amazing team at Grater Goods and Music 212 for holding down the fort so beautifully whilst my attention was split. Matt, Cary, Maki, Annika, Rosea, Max, Sonya, Sean, Charni, Rasa, Marco, Bene, El, Fynn, Youssef – you're all awesome.

Thanks to Sam Parish for helping us throughout the project – you're amazing and it was a pleasure to collaborate with you. Also to Lucinda and Belinda for editing and proofing the all-important recipes. Huge thanks to the Taylors for testing some stuff for us, in particular Laura for being so generous and kind. I also want to acknowledge the legends at Salut Salut. Lisa, Tessa and Kate – thanks for your energy, recipe ideas, love and wine. Enormous thank yous are also needed for my whānau, especially Mum, Helen and Papa G for their unfaltering support.

Merci Youssef and Anaïs for always being willing taste testers, je vous aime.

There doesn't need to be strict rules around food and life. We all just wake up every day and do the best we can, with the knowledge and resources we have. If you have enough food to eat, awesome! If you have the luxury of choosing what that is and where it comes from, make the choices that fit your ethics.

For me, food is a form of love and activism. And several times a day I get to love the people around me, animals and the planet through food. Not selflessly – I just love good food and once you learn that you can have all that pleasure whilst feeling smug as f*ck, why wouldn't you?

Flip x

Follow me and Grater Goods on social media for more plant-based meal ideas and recipes @gratergoods / gratergoods.co.nz / @flipgrater

KOA PRESS

Published in 2021 by Koa Press Limited.

www.koapress.co.nz

Director: Tonia Shuttleworth
Editor: Lucinda Diack
Sub-editor: Belinda O'Keefe
Designer: Tonia Shuttleworth
Photographer: Tonia Shuttleworth
Food stylists: Flip Grater & Youssef Iskrane
Prop stylist: Tonia Shuttleworth

A catalogue record of this book is available from the National Library of New Zealand.

ISBN 978-0-473-58769-7

Printed and bound in China by 1010 Printing.